THE NEW ADVENTURES OF
JAKE JETPU...

READING & MATH SKILLS
ACTIVITY BOOK

REVIEW

How well did you read the story? Answer the questions below:

1. Who took the Jewel of Wisdom ?

A. Jake
B. Marrz the Troll
C. Marvin thr Goblin

2. Who did the Jewel of Wisdom belong to?

A. Jake
B. Marrz the Troll
C. Julia

3. Where does Marrz want to start looking for the Jewel?

A. Drug Store
B. Donut Shop
C. Hotdog Cart

4. How does Jake distract Marvin the Goblin?

A. He yells at him
B. He hits Marvin with a strobe   blast from his eyes.
C. He makes faces at him.

WORD SCRAMBLE

Unscramble the words to reveal the secret message.

1. LYSAWA _____

2. OLLFWO _____

3. ORUY _____

4. MSAERD _____

MESSAGE:

_____   _____   _____   _____

SYLLABLES

A syllable is a single, unbroken sound of a spoken (or written) word. Syllables usually contain a vowel and accompanying consonants. Sometimes syllables are referred to as the 'beats' of spoken language.

For example:

water (wa/ ter) 2 syllables
cat (cat) 1 syllable
backpack (back / pack) 2 syllables

Clap as you say each syllable to identify the breaking sound between syllables.

			Syllables
Rainbow	Rain	bow	2
Hat			
Milkshake			
Skateboard			
Dog			
Football			

SUFFIXES

Suffixes are letters or groups of letters added to the ending of words to change their meaning. For example:

er = a person who
ful = full of
less = without

Sing + **er** = Singer (a person who sings)

Make words with the suffixes er, ful, and less.

EX:

		play	**ful**	**playful**
ful	play	_____	_____	_____
use	less	_____	_____	_____
er	box	_____	_____	_____
hope	ful	_____	_____	_____
climb	er	_____	_____	_____
less	pain	_____	_____	_____
ful	joy	_____	_____	_____

How many words can you make using the letters in

FEARLESS CHAMPIONS

_____   _____

_____   _____

_____   _____

_____   _____

JAKE JETPULSE™

©2018 JETPULSE COMICS™

JAKE JETPULSE™
LATER THAT DAY...
HEY GUYS! WHAT DO YOU WANT TO DO TODAY?
HEY JAKE! WE WERE ABOUT TO GRAB A BITE TO EAT...
THERE'S THAT TACO TRUCK...
WANNA JOIN US???
THE ONE BY THE BUS STOP??? COUNT ME IN!!!

REVIEW

How well did you read the story? Answer the questions below:

1. What time does Julia get out of school?

A. 12 noon
B. 3 PM
C. 2:30 PM

2. Where is the taco truck located?

A. Around the corner from Julia's school.
B. Near the bus stop.
C. In a shopping mall.

3. How did Julia get to school?

A. She ran all the way.
B. Marrz the Troll helped her.
C. She called a cab.

4. According to Marrz, what are they serving for lunch at Julia's school?

A. Pizza.
B. Tacos.
C. Cheeseburgers.

5. What caused Julia to run late for school ?

A. She missed her bus.
B. She overslept.
C. Street traffic.

PRACTICE

Solve the problems below. Then circle the correct answer.

1.

$3+4=$ _____

○ 7   ○ 6   ○ 8

2.

$5+5=$ _____

○ 12   ○ 10   ○ 15

3.

$6+3=$ _____

○ 4   ○ 9   ○ 11

4.

$9-4=$ _____

○ 5   ○ 7   ○ 3

5.

$8+4=$ _____

12   14   13

6.

$16-8=$ _____

○ 4   ○ 9   ○ 8

7.

$7-2=$ _____

○ 0   ○ 3   ○ 5

8.

$6-2=$ _____

○ 8   ○ 4   ○ 3

WORD PROBLEMS

Read the sentences below and answer each question.

Julia buys 10 apples from the store. She gives 4 apples to Marrz the Troll. How many apples does Julia have left?

_____ - _____ = _____

Julia walks 2 miles to the library. Then she walks another 2 miles to the movie theater. How many miles did she walk in all?

_____ + _____ = _____

Last week, Jake, Julia, and Marrz saved 5 boys and 2 girls from danger. How many kids did the they rescue last week?

_____ + _____ = _____

Marrz brought 10 stickers from the candy store. He loses 3 stickers on the way home. How many stickers does Marrz have left?

_____ - _____ = _____

COUNTING MONEY

Count the coins and write the amount.

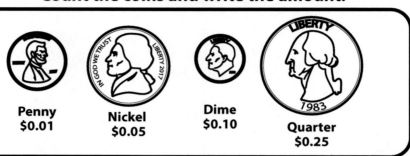

Penny
$0.01

Nickel
$0.05

Dime
$0.10

Quarter
$0.25

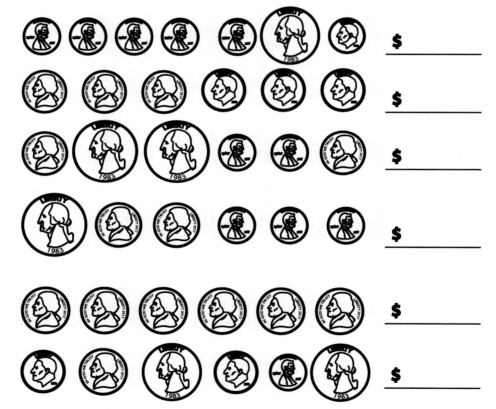

$ _____

$ _____

$ _____

$ _____

$ _____

$ _____

BEAT THE CLOCK

How many math problems can you solve in 2 minutes?

17 + 5 = ____   50 + 12 = ____

11 + 4 = ____   19 + 9 = ____

9 + 5 = ____   27 + 15 = ____

18 + 4 = ____   14 + 18 = ____

40 + 14 = ____   72 - 10 = ____

BEAT THE CLOCK!

How many math problems can you solve in 60 seconds?

14	12	18	16	12	17	12	11	19
- 7	- 3	- 9	- 5	- 6	- 9	- 7	- 8	- 9

20	14	24	8	6	16	11	9	24
- 5	- 5	- 3	+5	- 5	+16	+10	+7	+12

14	7	25	37	25	21	20
- 9	+5	+11	- 12	- 10	+25	- 11

LIGHTNING ROUND

10 + 7 = ____   8 + 4 = ____

12 + 2 = ____   7 + 7 = ____

4 + 3 = ____   9 + 8 = ____

6 + 6 = ____   5 + 5 = ____

9 + 5 = ____   9 + 9 = ____

WORD PROBLEMS

Read the sentences below and answer each question.

Marrz, Julia, and Jake order 15 tacos.
Moments later, they order 5 more.
How much did Jake, Julia, and Marrz eat altogether?

_____ + _____ = _____

Marrz, Julia, and Jake order 15 tacos.
Moments later, they order 5 more.
How much did Jake, Julia, and Marrz eat altogether?

_____ + _____ = _____

There are 4 girls in the library.
Moments later, 3 boys enter the library.
How many kids are there in all?

_____ + _____ = _____

Julia has 10 cookies. She gives 4 cookies to
her friend Lisa. How many cookies does
Julia have left?

_____ - _____ = _____

PRACTICE

Solve the problems below. Then circle the correct answer.

1.

$14 - 7 =$ _____

○ **4** ○ **6** ○ **7**

2.

$6 + 4 =$ _____

○ **8** ○ **10** ○ **9**

3.

$10 - 2 =$ _____

○ **6** ○ **8** ○ **9**

4.

$7 + 4 =$ _____

○ **11** ○ **12** ○ **10**

5.

$11 - 3 =$ _____

○ **9** ○ **7** ○ **8**

4.

$8 + 5 =$ _____

○ **13** ○ **12** ○ **11**

7.

$20 - 10 =$ _____

○ **10** ○ **9** ○ **11**

4.

$0 + 5 =$ _____

○ **5** ○ **0** ○ **4**

MULTIPLY BY 5

5 x 1 = ☐   5 x 7 = ☐

5 x 2 = ☐   5 x 8 = ☐

5 x 3 = ☐   5 x 9 = ☐

5 x 4 = ☐   5 x 10 = ☐

5 x 5 = ☐   5 x 11 = ☐

5 x 6 = ☐   5 x 12 = ☐

MULTIPLY BY 6

6 x 1 = ☐   6 x 7 = ☐

6 x 2 = ☐   6 x 8 = ☐

6 x 3 = ☐   6 x 9 = ☐

6 x 4 = ☐   6 x 10 = ☐

6 x 5 = ☐   6 x 11 = ☐

6 x 6 = ☐   6 x 12 = ☐

MULTIPLY BY 7

7 x 1 = ☐   7 x 7 = ☐

7 x 2 = ☐   7 x 8 = ☐

7 x 3 = ☐   7 x 9 = ☐

7 x 4 = ☐   7 x 10 = ☐

7 x 5 = ☐   7 x 11 = ☐

7 x 6 = ☐   7 x 12 = ☐

MULTIPLY BY 8

8 x 1 = ☐   8 x 7 = ☐

8 x 2 = ☐   8 x 8 = ☐

8 x 3 = ☐   8 x 9 = ☐

8 x 4 = ☐   8 x 10 = ☐

8 x 5 = ☐   8 x 11 = ☐

8 x 6 = ☐   8 x 12 = ☐

MULTIPLY BY 9

9 x 1 = ☐   9 x 7 = ☐

9 x 2 = ☐   9 x 8 = ☐

9 x 3 = ☐   9 x 9 = ☐

9 x 4 = ☐   9 x 10 = ☐

9 x 5 = ☐   9 x 11 = ☐

9 x 6 = ☐   9 x 12 = ☐

MULTIPLY BY 10

10 x 1 = ☐   10 x 7 = ☐

10 x 2 = ☐   10 x 8 = ☐

10 x 3 = ☐   10 x 9 = ☐

10 x 4 = ☐   10 x 10 = ☐

10 x 5 = ☐   10 x 11 = ☐

10 x 6 = ☐   10 x 12 = ☐

WORD PLAY

Write a sentence using each one of these sight words:

Strong	**Happy**	**Sad**
Force	**Young**	**Old**

1. _____

2. _____

3. _____

4. _____

5. _____

6. _____

JETPULSE ACADEMY
POWER ORBS

Use the sight words in the power orbs to complete the sentences below:

bright **around** **brave** **run** **mean**

1. Jake flies _____ town to find his friends.

2. Julia likes school. She is very _____.

3. Jake can _____ very fast.

4. Marrz is very _____.

5. Marvin the Goblin is _____ and grumpy.

USING THE NUMBER LINE

Use the number line to solve the problems.
Then write your answers in the blank lines below.

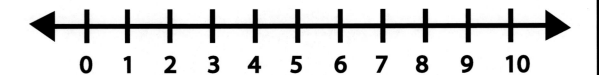

1. $4 + \underline{\hspace{1cm}} = 10$

2. $2 + \underline{\hspace{1cm}} = 8$

3. $6 + \underline{\hspace{1cm}} = 9$

4. $3 + \underline{\hspace{1cm}} = 6$

5. $7 + \underline{\hspace{1cm}} = 9$

6. $3 + \underline{\hspace{1cm}} = 5$

7. $2 + \underline{\hspace{1cm}} = 4$

8. $5 + \underline{\hspace{1cm}} = 7$

9. $4 + \underline{\hspace{1cm}} = 8$

10. $7 - \underline{\hspace{1cm}} = 3$

11. $10 + \underline{\hspace{1cm}} = 10$

12. $9 - \underline{\hspace{1cm}} = 8$

13. $4 + \underline{\hspace{1cm}} = 4$

14. $8 - \underline{\hspace{1cm}} = 3$

15. $6 - \underline{\hspace{1cm}} = 1$

WHAT TIME IS IT?

Draw the current time on the watch face below.

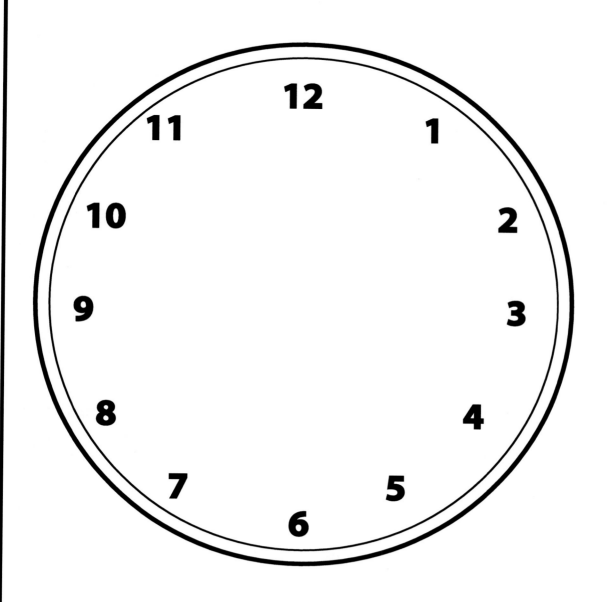

ODD OR EVEN?

Solve the math problems below.
Determine whether the sum is odd or even.

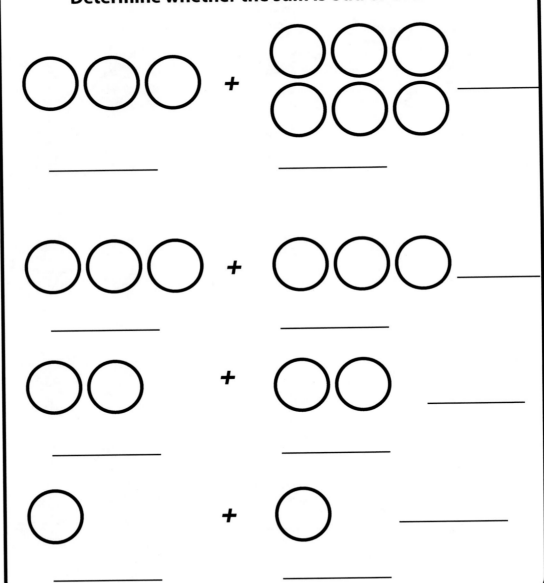

TRUE OR FALSE?

Marvin the Goblin has changed some
of the answers to the problems below.
Circle the ones that are true.

$7 + 5 = 14$ $\qquad$ $14 + 5 = 20$

$9 + 4 = 16$ $\qquad$ $16 - 3 = 13$

$8 + 5 = 13$ $\qquad$ $8 + 5 = 13$

$7 + 5 = 13$ $\qquad$ $13 + 5 = 19$

$5 + 4 = 10$ $\qquad$ $11 + 5 = 20$

$2 + 5 = 7$

$4 + 4 = 8$

$6 + 5 = 11$

$9 + 3 = 13$

$10 + 4 = 15$

EXPAND YOUR SKILLS

**Write the numbers in expanded form.
Then write the number word below it.**

Example:

525
___5___ Hundreds ___2___ Tens ___5___ Ones

Five hundred twenty five
_____

120
_____ Hundreds _____ Tens _____ Ones

_____

75
_____ Hundreds _____ Tens _____ Ones

_____

536
_____ Hundreds _____ Tens _____ Ones

_____

REVIEW

TRUE OR FALSE

7 + 5 = 14

9 + 4 = 16

8 + 5 = 13

7 + 5 = 13

5 + 4 = 10

SOLVE THE ADDITION PROBLEMS BELOW.

2 + 8 = _____

11 + 3 = _____

22 + 8 = _____

80 + 20 = _____

4 + 9 = _____

USE THE - OR + SIGNS TO MAKE EACH MATH SENTENCE TRUE.

15 _____ 5 = 20

40 _____ 12 = 52

16 _____ 9 = 7

50 _____ 24 = 26

Marrz brought 10 stickers from the candy store. He loses 3 stickers on the way home. How many stickers does Marrz have left?

_____ - _____ = _____

SCAMBLED SENTENCES

These sentences are not in order. Rewrite each sentence correctly.

FLY FAST. JAKE CAN VERY

_____

- -

_____

ARE BRAVE AND STRONG JAKE'S FRIENDS.

_____

- -

_____

STRONG AND WISE. IS JULIA

_____

- -

_____

AND PROTECT CITY. JAKE HIS FRIENDS THE

_____

- -

_____

ANSWERS:

1. JAKE CAN FLY VERY FAST.
2. JAKE'S FRIENDS ARE BRAVE AND STRONG.

3. JULIA IS SMART AND WISE.
4. JAKE AND HIS FRIENDS PROTECT THE CITY.

COMPOUND WORDS

Compound words are formed when two smaller words combine to form a new word. Here are a few examples:

Snow + ball: Snowball
Basket + ball: Basketball
Back + pack: Backpack

How many words can you make from the list below?

Break	**stand**	**kick**	**side**
fast	**camp**	**ground**	**site**
play	**man**	**snow**	**base**
ball	**base**	**foot**	**basket**

_____   _____   _____

_____   _____   _____

_____   _____   _____

_____   _____   _____

_____   _____   _____

_____   _____   _____

MARRZ
THE TROLL™

JAKE JETPULSE™

JAKE TO THE RESCUE!

JAKE JETPULSE™

JAKE JETPULSE™

JAKE JETPULSE™

MULTIPLY BY 3

3 x 1 =   3 x 7 =

3 x 2 =   3 x 8 =

3 x 3 =   3 x 9 =

3 x 4 =   3 x 10 =

3 x 5 =   3 x 11 =

3 x 6 =   3 x 12 =

JAKE JETPULSE™

JETPULSE ACADEMY
POWER ORBS

Use the sight words in the power orbs to complete the sentences below:

help   race   jump   fly   above

1. Jake is always happy to _____ his friends.

2. Julia likes to _____ her toy cars.

3. Marrz the Troll can _____ very high.

4. Jake can _____ high in the sky.

5. Jake can soar high _____ the clouds.

MULTIPLY BY 2

2 x 1 =

2 x 2 =

2 x 3 =

2 x 4 =

2 x 5 =

2 x 6 =

2 x 7 = ☐

2 x 8 = ☐

2 x 9 = ☐

2 x 10 = ☐

2 x 11 = ☐

2 x 12 = ☐

JAKE JETPULSE™

JAKE JETPULSE

AGE: 8 Years
Gender: Male
Height: 4 ft. 7 inches.
Birthplace: Bay Ridge, Brooklyn, N.Y.

Jake is like not like most boys. At a very young age, He was gifted with amazing super powers. With a strong and supportive family at his side, Jake learns **to use his magnificent abilities to protect the** citizens of earth.

At high altitudes, Jake can summon wormholes that allow him to travel anywhere within seconds. Jake can also manipulate the visible spectrum which is the portion of electromagnetic spectrum that is visible to the naked eye. At intense speeds, He can give the illusion that he is in multiple places at once.

Jake is a born leader. He prefers diplomacy over **aggressive conflicts. His inability to "read between the lines"** can be frustrating to those who do not know him. But gathers respect from his adversaries.

JULIA
THE SUPER GENIUS

Age: 11 Years
Gender: Female
Height: 4ft 11 inches
Birthplace: Sunset Park, N.Y.

When most kids her age are spending time at the movies or playing video games, Julia is firing up her Bunsen burner. She's more interested in chemistry, sci-fi novels, and competitive fighting robots. Julia enjoys spending time in the back of her uncle Leo's garage tinkering with old car engines. She's a great listener, but making friends is tough because she's intimidated by social interaction. Conversations can make her anxious unless the topics are related to science, math or history.

Like her hero, the famous physicist Albert Einstein, she owns several versions of the same blue and grey outfit because she prefers not to waste brainpower on choosing an outfit each morning.

Her oversized jacket belongs to her older brother, Victor. When Victor joined the military, Julia found it hard not having him around. To help her adjust to his absence, Victor left her to guard his high school varsity jacket. It's her security blanket. She's rarely seen without it.

Julia seems unaware that she possesses an incredibly high I.Q. New discoveries excite her and she's always eager to share new information with others. She believes in teamwork and she's always willing to help her friends.

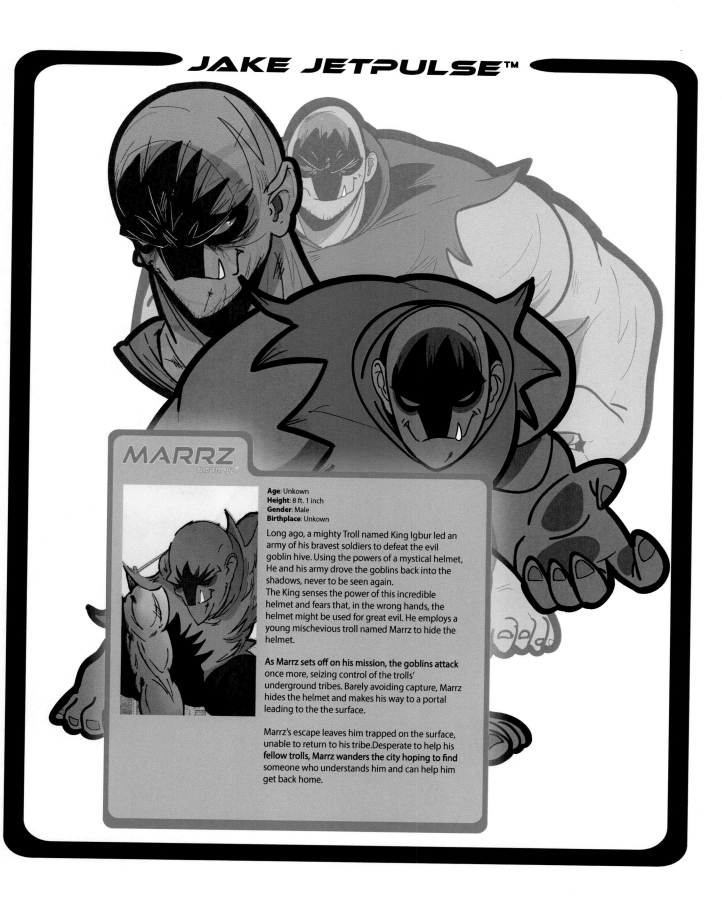

MARRZ
THE TROLL™

Age: Unkown
Height: 8 ft. 1 inch
Gender: Male
Birthplace: Unkown

Long ago, a mighty Troll named King Igbur led an army of his bravest soldiers to defeat the evil goblin hive. Using the powers of a mystical helmet, He and his army drove the goblins back into the shadows, never to be seen again.
The King senses the power of this incredible helmet and fears that, in the wrong hands, the helmet might be used for great evil. He employs a young mischevious troll named Marrz to hide the helmet.

As Marrz sets off on his mission, the goblins attack once more, seizing control of the trolls' underground tribes. Barely avoiding capture, Marrz hides the helmet and makes his way to a portal leading to the the surface.

Marrz's escape leaves him trapped on the surface, unable to return to his tribe.Desperate to help his fellow trolls, Marrz wanders the city hoping to find someone who understands him and can help him get back home.

JAKE JETPULSE™

JETPULSE

JAKE JETPULSE "HERO" SYMBOL TEE

Jake Jetpulse is more than a superhero. He is a symbol of equality and hope. Suit up and protect the world in style with authentic Jetpulse Comics apparel.

Price: $18.00

HTTPS://JAKEJETPULSE.COM/HERO-SHOP

©2018 Jetpulse Comics™

©2018 Jetpulse Comics™

Made in the USA
Middletown, DE
02 April 2021